RIPPED TO SHREDS

RIPPED TO SHREDS

A TRUE STORY OF DOMESTIC ABUSE IN A SMALL TOWN

Ann Wilson

iUniverse®

iUniverse books may be ordered through booksellers or by contacting:

iUniverse
1663 Liberty Drive
Bloomington, IN 47403
www.iuniverse.com
1-800-Authors (1-800-288-4677)

ISBN: 978-1-5320-2753-6 (sc)
ISBN: 978-1-5320-2749-9 (e)

Library of Congress Control Number: 2017910904

Print information available on the last page.

iUniverse rev. date: 04/12/2019

To the Father, the Son, and the Holy Spirit.
To my children, Ted, Marian, Tira, and Nicole, and my
grandchildren, who suffered with me yet comforted me.
To my parents, Ken and Doris, and my grandmother,
Debra, who took charge while I was healing.

To my siblings, Ken Jr. (deceased), Sara,
Tonya (deceased), Denise, Kelvin, and Toya.
To my aunts, uncles, nieces, nephews, cousins, and friends.
To every woman or man who has suffered, or is currently
suffering, with domestic violence. A tragic end can
be stopped in the beginning with awareness.

Purposed by God

There is a divine purpose for you.
Do not regret what you have gone through.
Others cannot see why.
There is a time set aside.
Your purpose will be known.
Hold on! Hold on!
You will survive.

Contents

Acknowledgments

I would like to give special thanks to the following people who have assisted me in the completion of this project. I appreciate your patience, understanding, and assistance. Thank you all for identifying with me, praying *with* me and *for* me before, during, and after this terrifying event that threatened to take over my life.

You all have been there when I needed you, and I can never thank you enough. Maybe you were there to lend a helping hand with typing my poems, helping me fill out paperwork, or translating materials for me. Whatever your role, please know that I will be forever grateful and you will always be in my heart.

To Candice Bray, Valerie Flowers, Darlene Holiday, Raven Harrison, Celeste Rivera, Nicole Blankenship, Lindsey Brown, Evelyn Bradley, Elizabeth Akens, Sue Taylor and Denise Jenkins -I love and appreciate you. To the medical staff at Lance-Madison Army Community Hospital, Colonel Andrews, and Nurse Henderson, I appreciate the extra special care you took in an effort to save my life. Hallelujah! It worked!

To the medical staff at Sims Thompson Medical Center and Doctors Henry, Avers, and Lauder, thank you for making those lifesaving decisions and sticking with me throughout these years.

I will never forget how safe I felt in your presence. Then assistant district attorney Alvin Campbell, Detective Raymond Owens, and Campbell's team of lawyers worked hard to secure a conviction, which was not easy back when domestic violence was such a taboo subject, so I thank them all for making sure my abuser did not escape justice.

Dr. Brad Costner for giving me the necessary tools for becoming a strong advocate against domestic violence. I thank everyone who sat down for interviews during the course of writing this book. Your input was valuable. Maybe you blessed me with a smile or a short conversation during those years when it was hard for me to look in the mirror. To you it might have been a small act, but to me it was everything! I thank you because I desperately needed to feel love.

Finally, I want to thank Emily Kirkley for her encouraging words.

Introduction

I am a survivor of domestic violence. I am writing this story to shed light on the devastation of domestic violence—and how it affected me and my children, my friends, my family, and other innocent people—in hopes that it will help others. By reading my story, you will understand what I experienced. Domestic violence is serious, and the abusers become bolder in carrying out their controlling plans. I had no idea that the man to whom I was married was an abuser. He hid all the obvious signs and masked them quite well. I suggest that people find out as much as possible about the individuals they become involved with. Consider background checks. Take your time instead of allowing your emotions to run wild. Look out for yourself, as well as your family and friends. The abuser cannot love. This is a proven fact. Commonly, the victim cannot comprehend why that person cannot love, but this is true. An abuser manipulates and controls. It will be his or her way and nothing else. Each one has a way to keep his or her victim under his or her control. The victim gives in and thinks that there is no hope. I felt the same way. I was placed in bondage, and that's what it felt like. I gave in to misery, helplessness, and hopelessness, and I just wanted to die. I lost my identity, the person God had made me to be. I was living under what my abuser wanted me to be. In my case, I felt there was nothing that could stop this abuse but death. But there is hope, help, and resources, such as the National Domestic Violence Hotline. Their number is 1-800-799-7233. It is open twenty-four hours, seven days a week, including holidays. They make referrals to place you into a safe environment. You can always call 911 too. I felt like I was at fault for the abuse, but this was not true. Each victim feels as though he or she has done something wrong to be abused. It is a normal reaction, but it is false. You are not at fault. I thought I could change him, but I could not. I did certain things that I thought would help him to see that I loved him, but it was to no avail. One cannot change the abuser. The only way to avoid the catastrophe of abuse is to seek help. That is a big start. It took years of counseling, hospitalizations, and surgeries after my husband shot me three times, which ripped half of the right side of my face off. I lost an eye, and I will always be in constant pain because of a nerve injury in my arm, not to mention the resection of fractured ribs from the bullets. I have bullet fragments all over my body that prevent me from having an MRI. I'm telling my story to help people realize that it is not over if they are involved in relationships with domestic violence. You can survive. You just need to get help and get out of it. You are not alone. I survived to tell my story so that others can take heed. There is light at the end of the tunnel, with faith and hope. Do not be ashamed of getting help. For those who are not involved in domestic violence situations, don't be afraid to make phone calls to the police or social services, especially if children are involved in the homes, if you suspect domestic violence. You could be saving someone's life. Remember that abusers cannot love. These people are cowards, and they strike unexpectedly. When I was growing up, I would see women with swollen black eyes, busted lips, and other injuries, and now I know that possibly they were victims of domestic violence. However, no one did anything for them. The law enforcement was not brought in, and these victims suffered in silence. Even at the time I was shot, the belief that women were at fault for the abuse was still pervasive. But now victims have a voice and can be heard. They can get the help and rehabilitation they need through resources available.

> The thief comes only to steal and kill and destroy; I
> came that they may have life, and have it abundantly.
> —John 10:10 NASB

Domestic violence is a national epidemic, one that continues to grow daily because victims are embarrassed or intimidated into silence, and those who surround the abused are hesitant to get involved for fear it will affect their own lives negatively.

Because of the silence, the abuser continues to control and abuse, and the victim continues to live in fear, oftentimes along with his or her children. The bystanders continue to stand by, waiting until something tragic happens that spins all of their lives out of control.

Inaction is what allows the horrific cycle of violence and abuse to continue to destroy families, individuals, and communities across the globe. The epidemic of abuse has grown and continues to rage on. One out of every three women and one out of four men will experience some form of physical violence in their lifetimes.

Women and children are suffering daily and oftentimes dying at the hands of their abusers. The countless names and faces of these victims may be unfamiliar to you. Maybe you've seen a story on the news or social media, but they are real people who are living day to day in the nightmare of abuse. Many of them lose their lives just as I almost did. These victims are real people, not fictional characters who are mourned for a week or two and then get back to *real* life. Nothing is that simple.

To millions across the world, *domestic violence is real*, and the victims are getting younger and younger. Every day young girls and boys are falling prey to abusers because no one is communicating with them about the possibility of coming across these abusive individuals.

To educate them, we must learn and become aware of the signs of abuse. We all must watch closely for warning signs. There are many small habits and traits an abuser may display early in the relationship that his or her potential victim may take as *cute signs of affection*. Consider the statement "If I can't have you, no one else will." This is not a sign of affection but a lethal threat that people should take seriously.

Things like jealousy, aggression, and control are some signs to look for. Oftentimes the abuser will want you to spend all of your time with him or her. If their intentions are pure, they will not want you to *stop* being around your friends or family members. This is called *alienation*.

My husband demanded no visiting and no visitors. He didn't want anyone close enough to realize what was going on. In the very beginning of our relationship, he also bought me clothes. He wanted me to dress a certain way. Abusers love being in control even down to the type of clothing you wear or the way you wear your hair.

They can hide the control under the guise of "I just wanted to buy you something nice" or "I want my girl/guy to look a certain way."

There's nothing wrong with having a preference, but forcing it on someone else is called *control*.

Verbal abuse is also a subtle way of exercising control. The abuser might say little things that have a big impact on an individual's self-esteem. My husband would often tell me, "Nobody wants a woman with children."

He wanted me to feel like I was lucky to have him. Criticizing or making fun of the victim chips away at his or her self-esteem, which causes depression, ego deflation, and the loss of self-dignity, self-worthiness, and self-respect. If negativity is reiterated long enough, a person will start to believe it. This happened to me. That was the abuser's intent.

The abuser does not like to be challenged. It threatens his or her control. I was cut by a bowl that my husband threw at me for asking why, and the wound required stitches to my hand. He would not allow me to go to the hospital. He told me it was my fault and that I had better use my own skills to stitch myself up. When I went back to work, I was questioned about it, but I made up a story and never told anyone the truth.

To cover what was happening, I quickly learned how to pretend and lie in that short six-week marriage. My coworkers were not crazy, and they knew something was wrong; however, they didn't pressure me to tell.

The young man who worked in personnel at the hospital questioned me when I went to change the beneficiary of my life insurance policy. I remember he told me, "Major Wilson, you've only been married three weeks. If you don't mind my saying so, that is too soon to change your beneficiary. You should really think about it."

I want my story to bring awareness of abuse and prompt victims to take action so that they can remove themselves from their abusers. Please visit the Domestic Violence website at http://www.ncadv.org and http://www.nrcdv.org for resources available.

To think that my husband had an ulterior motive as my insurance beneficiary was absurd. Subsequently, I found out that his plan was to kill me. I thanked the nice young man for his concern, but as I told him, "It's okay. He's my husband."

But it was not okay. My life insurance beneficiary should not have been a primary concern once I said, "I do."

Prologue

Ted

For the word of God is quick, and powerful, and sharper than any twoedged sword, piercing even to the dividing asunder of soul and spirit, and of joints and of marrow, and is a discerner of the thoughts and intents of the heart.

—Hebrews 4:12 KJV

Ted Wilson was five years old the day his mother, Ann, called him into the living room of their home. They had company, and she wanted him to come and say hello. Ted picked up the two action figures he had been playing with and ran into the living room.

When he rounded the corner, Ted immediately recognized the visitor standing next to his mother. He was the man who lived down the street from their home, and seeing him standing next to his mother made Ted visibly agitated.

He did not know the neighbor very well, but whenever he saw Jimmy, he became nervous.

"Ted, would you like to go next door to Jimmy's house and play?" asked Ann.

He hesitantly nodded his head.

"Come on, buddy," Jimmy said.

He took Ted by the hand and began walking out the door. The child turned back to look at his mother with a doubtful expression, but Ann was still smiling that huge smile.

Ted beckoned for his three-year-old sister, Marian, to come along.

Marian looked up at her mother for approval, and seeing her nod, she ran to catch her brother's hand. Together they walked out of the front door with Jimmy. Eventually, Ted confided in his mother. He expressed a fear that Jimmy would hurt her.

Ted also asked Jimmy, "Are you going to kill my mommy, are you?"

Jimmy responded, "I will never do anything to hurt your mother."

That turned out to be a lie.

Chapter 1

RIPPED TO SHREDS

Ann

You will not fear the terror of night, nor for the arrow that flies by day.

—Psalm 91:5 NIV

I stood at my front window and watched as the two police cars backed out of the driveway. I nervously shifted the weight from my right leg to my left, rubbing my forearm. As I glanced down at the tender spot on my left arm, I wondered if there would be a bruise this time.

We were both soldiers stationed at Fort Madison—Jimmy, a noncommissioned officer, and me, a registered nurse and commissioned officer.

My husband was a first sergeant, and he definitely didn't want that kind of negative attention. He was in charge of many soldiers and had an image to keep.

Each and every time he hit me, I prayed none of his licks would leave bruises, and they did. I could cover most of them with my uniform. My husband would regularly remind me, "You'd better not tell anyone what goes on in this house."

I heard my husband's voice over and over inside my head. So many times over the last four weeks he had spoken those words and told me he was going to kill me. I really feared what he would do if I dared to tell anyone. So instead of telling anyone, I suffered in silence, hoping this time would be the last time.

While we were dating, Jimmy would tell me I was beautiful and smart and how lucky he was to have me. He acted like I was the woman he had been waiting his whole life to meet. He never wanted to be apart from me. I thought we were a match made in heaven, but soon after marrying him, *everything* changed.

He started to call me ugly names; I was dumb and stupid so often that it felt like I was losing who I was, and with his constant criticism and abuse, my self-esteem plummeted. I really thought something was wrong with me. I thought if I made changes, it would make him love me.

I had this crazy idea that I had to alter the way I did things. Then maybe it would make a difference in the way he treated me, so I was constantly searching for answers. *Do I need to gain weight?* I thought. *Perhaps I need to change my hairstyle or dress differently? Maybe I need to learn how to cook better.* Some days I didn't know who I was or if I was going or coming.

I stopped talking to Jimmy unless he asked me a direct question because it was safer that way. It didn't take much to spark his anger, and I never knew what words were right to say. I *wanted* so desperately to communicate with my husband.

I wanted to talk like we did when we were dating. I believed if I was better and put forth more effort to please him, things in my marriage would get better. I tried, and the licks escalated.

As I stated before, we were both soldiers, so I figured *work* was a safe topic. We at least had some common ground. When he came home on the evening of March 18, 1992, I asked him a question, not intending to make him angry but simply to engage him in conversation.

"How's work today?" I asked.

Jimmy kept walking toward the hallway like he hadn't heard me. So I assumed he hadn't, and I repeated the question. He stopped walking, turned around, and descended on me so fast that I didn't have time to react.

Evidently, he took my question as a sign of disrespect. He got in my face and started yelling at me, telling me how sick he was of dealing with me and threatening to kill me. "I'm sick of you, Ann. You're hardheaded. I swear you gon' make me kill you one day. Don't you ever question me again. What's wrong with you? I ask you the questions. I don't answer to you!" Jimmy exclaimed.

I felt evil coming from him. He was angrier than I had ever witnessed.

It was about five o'clock. After asking him about his day, things took a U-turn unexpectedly. I didn't have time to respond. Jimmy grabbed me by the lapels on my shirt and dragged me across the room. My body hit everything in sight. The table fell on me, busting my head open. I started to bleed. I tried to explain what I meant; however, he was enraged, and there was no stopping him.

"Stop, Jimmy. Stop, Jimmy. I didn't mean to," I tried to explain.

He picked me up and rammed my head into the wall. He caught my neck and gripped around it with his bare hands. I could hardly breathe. When he released me, he said, "You don't question me. I ask the questions. You got that?"

I was so weak and exhausted. I asked God to give me strength. I made it to the kitchen and grabbed the knife I was using to cut up collard greens for dinner.

There was so much hatred in his eyes, and I was afraid. I had decided that he was not going to beat me anymore. He followed me into the kitchen but kept his distance once he saw the knife in my shaky hand. I watched his every move; determined not to let him get the upper hand again. He looked at me and shook his head in disgust. "What you gon' do with that knife, Ann, huh? What you gon' do? You'd better put that damn knife down."

He taunted me, but I didn't care. I stood there, shaking and crying, and if he tried to put his hands on me again, I was going to defend myself, or I was going to die in that house with my children. I was convinced that he was not going to leave anyone alive.

"Stay away from me, Jimmy. Stay away," I yelled.

Enough was enough. I reached over to pick up the phone while keeping an eye on Jimmy. He watched me closely as I took the receiver off the hook. Jimmy twisted his lips and sneered at me again.

"You'd better hang that phone up."

I shook my head to say no. I was tired of walking around my house on eggshells, scared to breathe. I didn't know when the licks were coming. I had to fight for me and my children. I became more determined to survive. I think he could see that.

With one shaky hand holding the knife, I held the phone receiver

3

with the other and threatened to call the police. "I'm going to call the police, Jimmy. Get out of my house."

Jimmy wasn't very tall in stature, but he was solid and heavy-handed. Compared to my five-foot, 110-pound frame, he was cosmic at five foot nine and 180 pounds.

In that moment, he stood across from me, looking like he could kill me with his bare hands. He had proven that he did not love me. Although I was afraid of him, I could not continue to be his punching bag.

"Get out of here, Jimmy, and leave me alone, or I'm going to call the police."

Jimmy laughed at me, turned, and walked out of the room, but not before giving me a final warning. "You'd better not call the police."

I don't know if I really intended to call the police when I picked up the phone, but once I held that phone in my hand and repeatedly said that I was going to call them, I felt empowered. I felt strong, and before I knew it, I had dialed the number. There was no turning back now. I had finally found the courage to fight back and while it started a hailstorm of grief and sorrow that would continue for years and years to come, I'm still glad that I took that first step.

Chapter 2

A CRY FOR HELP

My dear brothers and sisters, take note of this:
Everyone should be quick to listen, slow to speak
and slow to become angry, because human anger
does not produce the righteousness that God desires.
—James 1:19–20 NIV

When the operator responded, "This is 911. What's your emergency?" I asked for help, and I prayed they would come and take Jimmy away forever because *I* knew if he ever returned, he would make good on his threats. In my heart, I knew he would kill me. I had openly defied him.

He had said it too many times not to really mean it, and after I got the knife to defend myself, I knew there was no reversing what had taken place. I was certain he wouldn't hesitate to kill me if he got the opportunity, but I wasn't going to give him the chance. I had already called the police, so I counted on the fact that they were on the way.

After I hung up the phone, I yelled down the hallway to Jimmy. I wanted him to know what I had done, hoping it would scare him and he would just get his things and leave. "Jimmy, get out of here. The police are on the way," I said.

When I got no response, I took the knife and quietly walked down the hallway. I could see the bedroom door was closed.

I stood outside the door for a little while longer, listening. It seemed as though he was looking for something. I knew he had a sawed-off shotgun and a .45 Magnum that he kept in the bedroom. The door was closed.

He's looking for the guns, I thought.

I didn't know what he was doing inside the bedroom.

I yelled Jimmy's name through the door and banged on it a few times, but he still did not respond. In frustration and fear, I took the knife and jammed it in the door. I could hear Jimmy moving around inside the room at that point, so I yelled Jimmy's name again. "Jimmy, you can't stay here anymore. "The police are on their way." I was afraid but no one could hear my cry.

I was crying. I poured out all the frustration and pain that had been building up over the past weeks. I had tried everything I could to make the marriage work. I was so tired of living under abusive and violent circumstances that I had no interest in living.

The police arrived in a nick of time. I felt that Jimmy had found the gun. Everything in the background had quieted except a clicking sound. If they had not come at the right time, I would have been dead. I was still very emotional and upset upon their arrival, so they took a moment and allowed me to calm down, and then they went to speak with my husband. Jimmy came out of the bedroom after they identified themselves, and the first thing he did was show the police the spot where I had stuck the knife in the door.

Of course, he tried to turn the tables and act like he was the victim. Jimmy told them I was crazy and had tried to attack him with the knife. However, he had no visible signs of an attack, but of course, I did. Because of this, they told him that he had to vacate the home and that he needed to follow them to the police department.

My husband was not arrested at the house. I know this because they did not put him in handcuffs. He drove his personal vehicle, so I do not know definitely that he went to the police department or if he was just removed from the home for the time being. I only know they *told him* to follow them to the police station.

As with many victims of abuse, I was embarrassed and ashamed of what had been going on inside my home, but I told the police everything, not that I had to say a single word. They could see the chaos—the overturned table with books scattered everywhere, the broken chair by the window, and the holes in the wall from Jimmy throwing things.

I had bruises around my neck, head, and other marks in various stages of healing. I was battered and abused, and the only thing I desperately wanted was to figure out what I had to do to end this nightmare of a marriage and move on with my life.

I was scared of what Jimmy would do if he came back home, but I was glad that I finally mustered up the courage to speak out and fight back. It was so exhausting carrying the weight of abuse in silence.

I had come to the realization that if I continued to allow him to hit me, he would continue to do it. Some miraculous change wasn't going to come over him so that he decided to be a better man. He was an abuser, and I knew things were not going to change unless I sought out help.

At that point, I believed I had done my part by calling the police because they were the only ones who could stop him. I genuinely believed that. If they didn't do anything to help me, I knew eventually he would kill me and my children. We had too much to live for.

I was embarrassed to admit that I had made a horrible mistake marrying Jimmy. To this day, I regret allowing our relationship to move so quickly. That is a mistake a lot of people make. They don't take the time to get to know their partners before sharing their values.

My relationship with my husband was too much too soon, and in retrospect, I know if I had taken a little more time to get to know him, I would have seen him for who he really was and not who he pretended to be. The abuse began immediately after the marriage. First, it was verbal, then he started hitting me.

Perhaps, if I had made him wait, he would have seen that I wasn't going to take any wooden nickels. Then he may have moved on and sought out someone else. But had that occurred, there would have been another poor soul in my shoes, so that would not have solved the problem of his abusive behavior.

Perhaps, if I had listened to the discernment of my parents, March 18, 1992, would not have been a display of terror that night. Both of my parents' words still echoed in me, "Ann, don't marry him. Something is not right."

But I do know God makes no mistakes. He knew us before we were born. He made me who I am, so He knew my strengths as well as my weaknesses. He also knew the issues Jimmy had.

My only hope is that my story has not been in vain and that it will be a blessing for others who bear the shame of domestic abuse. I pray at least one young lady or man will read my story and recognize signs and behaviors of the abuser, and will make better choices than me. None of us deserve to be battered and abused, and that is why I am speaking out and sharing my experience.

With this story, I hope to reach out and save one woman or man from the pain and suffering that nearly paralyzed the lives of me and my children. Love does not hurt.

Wife

I am your wife, and from you I came—by a rib taken by God
From the side of man.
I am your help meet, companion, to see you through.
We are as one, not that of two.
As I love you in holiness, God has joined.
Never to be your footstool to rest your feet upon,
Not to be your head, as king upon a throne.
I am virtuous and to my husband a crown—
And to make ashamed is as rottenness is in his bone.

Chapter 3

DECEPTION

And the serpent said unto the woman, ye shall not surely die.

—Genesis 3:4 KJV

When I met him on December 4, 1991, Jimmy pretended to be the perfect gentleman. He would often take me out to dinner and buy me nice things—clothes, flowers, and sweet perfume—tell me how beautiful I was and how he wanted to take care of me and my children, and my little heart would melt.

I was a single mother, and I was also a soldier, so my life was full of responsibilities. There were times when I felt lost in the shuffle, trying to balance my nursing job with being a good parent.

Everything in my life was a priority except me, so I appreciated the attention Jimmy showered me with. It was like water and sun raining down on a withered flower.

It felt good having someone who was willing to take care of my needs for a change. He always seemed concerned about my welfare. Was I getting enough rest? Had I eaten dinner? I soon found myself falling for him, even though I was not physically attracted to him initially.

He always wore a short, neat brush cut, and he dressed nicely too. He was so nice and kind to me and my children, and I liked that.

And more important than anything, he *feigned* interest in my children. To me, he was the perfect guy, showering us with love and affection. He took my kids under his wing and treated them like his own, asking to spend time with them. There was plenty of laughter and some fun days when he would take Ted riding with him. I later found out that my son always harbored a dislike for Jimmy. Jimmy's eyes, he mentioned, always scared him.

Ted stated there were many times when he would look at Jimmy and something would tell him, "You have to warn Mommy. He's going to hurt her." But at the time, I thought he was a godsend. I couldn't see anything but the smiles he brought to my face. I was in love.

After a couple of months, we were in a full-fledged relationship, and I began envisioning a future with him. Jimmy constantly talked about marriage, telling me he couldn't wait to make me his wife, and we talked about building our family. I fell head over heels in love with him and couldn't wait to become his wife.

Prior to our meeting, I was in the process of purchasing my first home, and when I closed on my house, we decided that a few months later we should go ahead and move in together. We had already made plans to marry, so we figured it wouldn't hurt anything. We could save money on rent and begin our lives together.

I knew I was not doing the right thing by allowing him to move in because my parents would not approve of us shacking up, so I allowed him to move in and simply did not tell them. I was afraid they would find out anyway, so instead of taking our time to get to know each other, we quickly set a date and decided to go ahead and get married.

I remember the day Jimmy, the kids, and I rode to Mississippi for him to meet my parents. I was excited to take my fiancé home because I was sure everyone would love him as I did, but after they met, I looked into my daddy's eyes and saw a look that was unfamiliar to me.

It was almost as if my daddy was afraid. I couldn't understand what he saw in my fiancé that made him so uncomfortable. My father was one of the bravest men I knew, but when it came to this relationship, I couldn't or wouldn't see what he saw.

I was too excited about finally meeting someone who loved me and wanted to make me his wife, not his girlfriend or his woman on the side. He wanted to marry me despite the fact that I already had a family. Being unmarried and having children was taboo, and I worried too much about what others thought of my status as a single parent.

After we left Mississippi, I wasn't so sure about my pending marriage. Both of my parents had expressed reservations about Jimmy, and that made me feel unsettled. But despite *my* nervousness, Jimmy didn't miss a beat. He continued to be my loving fiancé, putting my reservations at ease.

I felt like it was too late to back out anyway. We were already living together. Even when the pastor I had chosen to marry us refused to perform the ceremony without giving me an explanation, I moved forward with my plans.

I would be lying if I said I wasn't worried because I was a little bit apprehensive, but I really thought I was in love, and eventually everyone would see Jimmy for the wonderful man he was as I did.

Over the years, I have had to deal with myself and stay true to me. After the day we drove to Mississippi to meet my family—we ended up coming back home the very same day too—I had a little uncertain feeling that I pushed to the back of my mind. Periodically, I questioned myself, *Am I doing the right thing?*

Right up until the minute I walked into the courthouse, I wondered if I was doing the right thing. My parents' reservations, and the change in wedding plans had really shaken me up. I was so confused about what to do because I really couldn't see the danger they saw. I asked myself, *Should I break off the engagement because everyone can see something that I don't?*

I only saw the good in Jimmy. But I was still a little concerned because I knew my parents were very wise people. I also know they had never been quick to judge anyone harshly, but they had done so with my fiancé. So yes, I was worried because I wanted everyone to like him.

I trusted my parents' judgment unequivocally, even though I thought they were a little bit old-fashioned in their ways. The problem was I didn't know how to stop the roller coaster without having to abandon the whole ride, so I tried to put their concerns out of my mind and instead concentrated on enjoying the journey.

I was willing to do whatever I had to do to make the relationship work, so I followed my heart all the way to the courthouse, and on February 2, 1992, I married who I thought was the man of my dreams.

The moment I said, "I do," I looked into my husband's eyes and thought I could see *forever*, but that feeling was very short-lived. I realized I was in trouble shortly after the ceremony was over as we were leaving the courthouse. My husband immediately showed his true colors and began shedding his persona right before my eyes. There was no eventual descent into neglect and abuse. It started immediately.

The coldness my father spoke about became apparent as we walked down the courthouse steps. I was all giddy and giggly with stars in my eyes. I thought we were about to honeymoon and start our lives as husband and wife when he abruptly let the wind out of my sails!

"I don't have time for that mess. I'm going riding with my friends. I'll see you later," Jimmy said.

I had suggested a romantic dinner for just the two of us, but he looked at me like I disgusted him and dismissed me like I was a pesky gnat instead of his new bride.

I was beyond hurt, but I put my feelings to the side, went home, and carried on with business as usual. After his late return, he showered, went to bed, and refused to touch me. I was stunned at his complete 360-degree turn, but I kept silent, not wanting to upset or further alienate him. This was his first time rejecting me, and it would not be his last.

Very early in the marriage, I found myself in the midst of a nightmare of abuse. My husband began treating me like I was in his way, and his rejection confused me and affected my ego. I could not understand why he was always angry with me for no apparent reason. I just prayed that he would tell me about whatever I was doing to make him angry so that I could fix it.

He began to lay down all these rules, telling me what I could and could not do and what I could and could not say to him. He would refer to his rank as if I was one of his soldiers. I knew deep in my heart that I wasn't doing anything to anger him, yet he was constantly lashing out at me.

My mind started playing tricks on me. I thought I had done something wrong. I started questioning myself and *my* sanity.

The first time he hit me, I had broken one of his rules. He told me I could not look him in the eyes, and of course, I looked at him in disbelief. When I did, he grabbed me around the throat and banged my head into the wall.

I was so scared when he grabbed me that I almost *lost* it. A few nights later as I was passing by the spot, I looked at the wall and noticed a long nail protruding a mere three inches from the place where he had banged my head. I felt a chill all over my body because I could see a long strand of my hair hanging from the nail. What would've happened if my head had hit that nail? The answer made the hairs on both of my arms stand up.

I felt like I was living in the midst of a bad dream, but I was not the only one who suffered in that house. Immediately, my husband stopped playing with my children, laughing with them, and spending any type of quality time with them. He basically ignored their existence.

Although we were both soldiers, we worked different schedules. He worked from 9:00 a.m. to 5:00 p.m., and I went in at night from 10:00 p.m. to 8:00 a.m. He would not allow me to leave my children in his care at night while I worked. In fact, he forced me to take them to a babysitter's house. Truthfully, I was scared to leave them with him anyway.

One night, I called the house from my job for no particular reason just to chat. I was constantly trying to find ways to improve my marriage. Jimmy answered the phone and told me not to call there unless it was an emergency. I couldn't believe he had the nerve to forbid me to call my own house. He made it perfectly clear that he didn't have anything to say to me.

My husband no longer felt like he had to pretend to be in love with me. He had me where he wanted me. I was hurt, but I stayed out of his way and just made sure I kept my children out of his way as well. I began tiptoeing around the house, afraid of angering him, but it didn't work. He was always angry for some reason or another.

Chapter 4

AN ILL WIND BLOWS

Therefore put on the full armor of God, so that when the day of evil comes, you may be able to stand your ground, and after you have done everything, to stand.

—Ephesians 6:13 NIV

On March 18, 1992, I had taken the first step. I had finally made up my mind that I was not going to walk around my own home, scared to breathe. I was not going to allow my husband to abuse me another day. He would not punch me in my stomach, kick or slap me, ram my head into the wall, or drag me around and leave me with a bruised body.

After he left with the police, my heart was so heavy with grief and pain that I could barely carry its weight. Tears flowed like a river so much that it scared me. I thought about what had just taken place and more surprisingly, my response to defend myself.

I walked into the bathroom and closed the door because I didn't want my children to come out of the room and see me crying. I sat down on the toilet seat, and the dam broke.

Once the tears started rolling, I could not hold them back. I tried to stop crying, but I couldn't seem to get myself under control.

I did not hear the bathroom door open when my five-year-old son, Ted, walked in and looked up at me with frightened eyes. He grabbed my hand, tugging slightly. "Come on, Mommy. We have to go. We have to leave here. He's gonna kill you."

His words cut me to the core. I wiped my eyes and looked down at him. He was such a smart and caring little boy, and he shouldn't have had to carry the weight of my abuse at his age.

I got myself together and gave him a big hug. I held his small hand in mine and mustered up as much cheer as I could and told him it was going to be okay. I reassured him, "No, sweetie, he's not going to kill me. You don't have to worry about that."

Ted continued to look at me with those frightened eyes, and I have to admit that I wasn't as confident as I was pretending to be. But if we left, where could we go? This was our home. Plus, none of my friends or family knew what we had been going through. Who would be willing to take in a woman with two small children and possibly have to deal with a stalking abuser placing everybody's lives in jeopardy? I dismissed the notion, trying to convince myself that my words held credibility.

"Come into the kitchen and help me cook dinner, Ted," I said.

I stood up and looked in the mirror and quickly tried to tame my hair. I washed my face with a warm washcloth and stared at my reflection in the mirror. The eyes that stared back at me looked shell-shocked. I was a mess. I grabbed Ted's hand, turned, and walked out of the bathroom.

We walked across the hallway into the bedroom to check on my three year old daughter. I reached over and tucked the blanket tightly under my baby girl's chin, thankful that she had slept through the *last* fight.

If I had my way, this was going to be the last time my son would be scared and forced to sit quietly while I endured abuse at the hands of *my husband*. Both of my children had witnessed the abuse.

As the greens boiled in the pot, I reached down into the cabinet and pulled out a skillet to fry some pork chops. I thought, *Maybe me and my kids can have a nice, quiet dinner for a change.* I poured oil into the pan. I imagined how nice it would be without having to eat in silence or censor my conversation.

My husband's house rules were a real burden. I couldn't ask him any questions, and I couldn't make any statements without making him angry. I was imprisoned, and I felt like he was getting me ready for *the* kill.

He had this rule that I could never look him in the eye, and after being knocked to the floor so many times; I stopped looking at him altogether. I started walking around with my eyes down for fear I would get hit if I broke the rule.

15

I was thankful that the police had taken Jimmy away. But as relieved as I was that he was gone, I couldn't help but worry about how long the police were going to keep him. Was he locked away? Would they release him so that he could come back and finish what he started?

I prayed that he would not come home, but the nervous sinking feeling that settled in the pit of my stomach told me something different. The mere thought of having to see him gave me *anxiety*. Determined to push through, I focused my concentration on preparing dinner for my family.

An hour later, I was flouring the pork chops when the door to the garage swung open. I turned away from the counter and looked directly at my *husband*. I immediately lowered my eyes and began to shake, but he just stared at me with contempt and did not say anything.

I quickly turned to the stove and began stirring my greens. I had to do something with my hands because they had begun to visibly shake. I didn't want him to see the terror in my eyes or my hands shaking because I knew how much he enjoyed seeing me helpless and afraid. It seemed the more fear I showed, the better it made him feel, and I did not want to give him any more ammunition to use against me.

Only a few feet separated us, and I could feel his anger take over the small kitchen area. It was almost palpable. He was going to kill me. I could literally feel death again surrounding me, and I had no idea what I could do to stop it. It was like being on a roller coaster. I just didn't know how to slow it down or stop it. I felt like I had to ride it out until the end. And sadly, I knew the end could mean *death*.

"You just got me a police record." Jimmy said the words so calmly that it frightened me even more because as simple as those words were, they were said with finality, and I could literally hear the words his mouth did not say. It was those words—the unspoken ones—that shook me to the core.

"You're going to pay for calling the police," Jimmy said.

The threat hung in the air like a bad omen. As he walked past me to go down the hallway, my whole body began to shake uncontrollably. I didn't know what he was going to do, but I stood at the counter and just prayed. He came back into the kitchen and headed toward the door. But before he walked out, he made a declaration that should've given me some peace, but I wasn't convinced. "I'm leaving. Gotta get the hell outta here. I will be back to pack my things."

When he slammed the door shut, I let out the breath I had been holding in. He said he was going to leave, but that statement did not make me feel better. I did not believe him because my heart was telling me something different.

I leaned on the counter for support. My heart was beating so fast I could feel it pounding through my chest. I could hear it vibrating in my ears, and I didn't know what to do.

I had already called the police one time, and he came back. I could not understand his return. His anger had reached another level, and I was going to pay the ultimate price.

I reached into the cabinet for a tall water glass and poured myself a drink of the cognac Jimmy kept in the kitchen cabinet.

As I stood against the counter, drinking the hot liquid, I couldn't help thinking to myself how correct my father had been when he had said, "There's something not right about that man, Ann."

I poured another drink and quickly swallowed it as I thought about that day. My hands shook as I remembered my daddy's words. How true they had been. But on this day after my husband walked out of the door, leaving a deathly chill in the air, I could clearly understand the frightened look in my father's eyes. He was afraid for me. He feared for my life.

As I prepared dinner for my family on that dreary evening, I remember thinking back to my wedding day. Six weeks ago I had stood in front of the magistrate judge. No, *we* had stood in front of the magistrate judge and pledged our love, but he hadn't meant a word of our vows, not one.

We had promised *to have and to hold, for better, for worse, for richer, for poorer, in sickness and in health and to love and to cherish till death do us part.* As I stood at the stove, preparing dinner plates, I thought to myself, *I guess this is the "for worse" part.*

I was ready and willing to be a good wife. Why wasn't that enough to make my husband feel the same way? Why wasn't it enough for him to keep his hands off me in anger. Surely, constantly instilling fear into the lives of me and my children and unleashing his rage was not the love I so desperately wanted for me and my children.

As I sat down at the table to eat dinner, I had no idea what kind of storm was brewing outside, and even if I had had a million years to plan, I still would not have been prepared for what was to come in the next few minutes. Never in my most terrifying nightmare could I imagine the worst-case scenario of my wedding vows would become my reality.

Never mind the "for worse" part. I could survive that. It was the other part that turned my life upside down and set me on such a tumultuous path of grief and adversity that some days I would wish to leave this world behind. My husband's anger and vengeance would soon make the phrase "Till death do us part" my gruesome reality.

I Am Special to God Too!

I am special to God, just like you,
And was not placed on earth to be used and abused.
You slapped me in the face, and I turned the other cheek.
You slammed my body to the floor
Because you thought that I was weak.
You placed bullets in my body that tore it all apart
Because you thought that I was not special to God.
My children witnessed what I was going through,
So I sought counseling for them all because of you.
I thought you loved me the same as I loved you;
Instead, I received footprints from your shoe.
But one day you will pay and stand steadfast in your place
Because I am a woman special to God,
An ornament of His grace.

Chapter 5

A CLOUD ON THE HORIZON

And do not fear those who kill the body but cannot
kill the soul; but rather fear Him who can destroy both
soul and body in hell (Gehenna).
                                                    —Matthew 10:28 AMPC

"Get up," a voice whispered in my ear. "Get up now." I dropped my
fork and hesitantly looked around the kitchen, trying to figure out
where the cryptic warning had come from. Mirian was kneeling in
her chair next to me, eating a piece of corn bread with her fingers,
and her brother was sitting next to her, slowly eating his food. So I
knew neither of them had spoken.

I stood up from the table. I prayed that it was not my husband,
but I saw no one else in the room. I pushed my chair under the table
and walked slowly toward the living room.

With each step I took, my heart sank further. My heartbeat went
into overdrive, and I began to perspire. My forehead, armpits, and
my neck became moist with apprehension and anxiety. It was my
greatest fear that I would round the corner to the living room and
my husband would be standing there, still angry that I had called
the police on him, but I knew I had to eventually face him, so I willed
my body to keep moving.

Right before I rounded the corner, I heard a loud banging sound,
and the kitchen door swung open and slammed against the chair
where my son sat eating. I turned around, surprised and terrified at
the same time. Standing in the doorway was my worst nightmare.
I opened my mouth to say something, anything, but there was
nothing. My mouth became numb like it was stuffed with cotton.
My lips moved, but not one sound escaped.

In that instance, I stood facing my tormentor, my abuser, the man who pledged to love me until death, and I was terrified because I knew I was staring into the eyes of *death*. He had told me on more than one occasion to never look him in the eyes, and there I was, standing there totally vulnerable and afraid, staring into the dark, evil eyes of this person I did not know, the man who wanted to make me pay for calling the police.

I wanted to look away or blink and have him disappear—anything to make him go away, but I was powerless to move. I stood there for what seemed like a lifetime, facing him, but I know that in reality only a few seconds elapsed.

There was no time to think, no time to take a deep breath, just a moment in time when everything happened in slow motion and I could only stand in wonder. It was almost as if *life* knew I had reached the end and decided to press the pause button to give me a moment to reflect on what bought me to this point.

If you have never faced a traumatic event like this one where I saw my entire life pass in front of my face in a matter of seconds, it might be hard for you to understand what I am describing here. I can only say in that short moment, I saw the same eyes my daddy saw. I saw Pastor Hill's refusal to marry us, and I saw my heart's hesitation. And *yes*, I saw the frightened eyes of my son, who had tried to tell me on more than one occasion. I saw the signs that were all laid out for me. How he pulled me in with his nice guy routine.

Jimmy professed his love for me and my children. He acted like I was the woman he had been waiting for his entire life, and he pressured me to change the beneficiary of my life insurance policy to his name instead of my children's names. He had tried to force me to add his name to the deed to my house.

Standing there, I could see that he was looking for a reason to kill me from day one. In that short moment, I fully comprehended that I was facing a powerful and indescribable evil force. My husband no longer looked like a person to me. All I could see was the dark, sinister eyes that seemed like dead black pools of evil determined to *steal* my life.

In that moment, standing in my dining room, everything blacked out except me, the gun, and thankfully, the power of my God!

"Ann, didn't I tell you I was going to kill you?" Jimmy looked at me and spat out the most terrifying words I had ever heard, although he had said them many times before. The fact that he was pointing a huge black gun directly at me made the reminder even more frightening.

Before I could think, move, or exhale, I heard the crack of the .45 Magnum and saw a blinding flash of light. I felt an excruciating pain rip through the soft flesh of my face, knocking me against the dining room wall, blowing off the right side of my face. A power arose inside of my body unlike I never felt before.

Before I could comprehend what was happening, a second bullet sent a wave of heat through my shoulder blade, incapacitating my left arm. I actually saw my arm *expand* and *contract* like something out of a science fiction movie, and I knew the bullet had struck a nerve.

Oh Lord, what is happening to me? He is trying to kill me, I thought as I turned my body in an attempt to flee while silently screaming on the inside. The bullets whizzed by softly, but they tore up everything in their wake. I stopped and leaned on the wall to catch my breath as my attacker closed the distance between us.

"Didn't I tell you I was going to kill you?" Jimmy reminded me again of his threat as he shoved the gun into my rib cage and followed me into the hallway and leaned into my body. He pulled the trigger for the third time, leaving my body limp and spilling blood from the bullet holes.

As I tried to move, blood poured from my body, leaving a bloody trail. My last vision of my husband was the bottoms of his boots heading down the hallway toward the bedrooms. As I collapsed on the floor, everything around me seemed foggy. I could barely believe what had just taken place. My husband had shot me. *He shot me!*

My body was wracked with pain, and I could not see out of my right eye. My face felt as if it was melting, and my skin burned with an intense fire.

I thought I had been shot in the brain, but fortunately, that was not the case because I was still conscious and aware of my surroundings. There was so much blood and gore oozing out of me and covering my face that I knew I was only moments away from death.

My children, I thought as my body began to heave violently. As I strained to look out of my left eye, I knew immediately that the bullet to my ribs had collapsed my lungs. My vomit looked thick and brown like ground coffee. Having graduated from Howard University with a nursing degree, I knew exactly what the ground coffee vomitus meant. If I didn't move my body to an upright position, I would *drown* in my own blood.

Dragging myself into the living room, I half-walked and half-crawled with one arm into the green chair by the front window. I was in so much pain, and I was acutely aware that my right eye was no longer attached and was hanging out of its socket.

My breathing became shorter and shorter as I tried to force myself to sit up in the chair, but I could not get to an upright position. I was lying slumped over the arm of the chair with my left arm hanging limp and useless. I knew that position was not going to help keep me alive, and I desperately wanted to live.

Get up, Ann, I prodded myself. I knew I had to try harder to get to a sitting position, or I was going to die just like my husband had planned. *But I wanted to live!* I wanted to watch my children grow up. I wanted to see little Ted grow up, go to school, and play Little League sports. I wanted to see him wearing his cap and gown when he was graduating.

I wanted to see Marian grow up and go to her high school prom, get married, and have children of her own. I didn't want to die in the middle of my living room. Not here, not in the house I had purchased a few months earlier and patiently decorated and prepared for my children's first home. I did not want to die here. This would not be the last vision my children had of me.

My children? Where are my children? I stood up from the chair, amazed that I was able to stand. The chair was saturated with my blood and pieces of my flesh. I was amazed that I was able to focus and think. *How am I thinking, Lord?* I was shot in the head and parts of my face were plastered against the dining room wall and the china cabinet, but somehow I was still able to reason.

Go, Ann. Move, I told myself as I stumbled into the dining area and sunk down onto the small couch in front of the door, thankful that I had insisted on keeping it when Jimmy decided that he would be moving his furniture in my house and giving the rest of my furniture to his aunt.

Sitting up on my couch, I stared out of my left eye at the kitchen table where I had been feeding my children. Looking at the food left on the table, my mind raced a hundred miles a minute. *Where is he? Where are my children? Has he hurt them too? Lord, this was not the life I had planned. This was not supposed to happen to me. What did I do to bring this kind of pain and suffering into my home?*

Silently, I cried on the inside. For fear he would come and finish me off, I remained silent on the outside, but on the inside I screamed with the intensity of a person who was paralyzed as the blood drained from my body one ounce at a time.

I cried at the injustice. I was in so much pain. I was *dying!* I was dying, and the only thing I could do was sit on my couch and wait as life seeped quickly from my body. I leaned back and closed my eye and concentrated on breathing.

"I shot my wife." I heard Jimmy's voice, but I lay there, barely breathing; not daring to look at him. I was afraid he was going to shoot me again. I hadn't heard the gun discharge again, and I never heard my babies cry. And even in the midst of dying, that made my heart rejoice.

Someone was coming, and God willing, my children were safe somewhere. Help was on the way. Praying that I would continue to live and he had not hurt my children as he had done me, I finally succumbed to the *darkness.*

The Breath of Life

Each breath we take is not on our own—
It is God that is in control.
He formed man from the dust of the ground
And breathed into his nostrils
The breath of life,
And man became a living soul.
Each breath we take is because of God's love,
A gift and a blessing to never take for granted.

Chapter 6

WHEN IT RAINS

The LORD is with me; I will not be afraid. What can mere mortals do to me? The LORD is with me; he is my helper. I look in triumph on my enemies. It is better to take refuge in the LORD than to trust in humans.

—Psalm 118:6–8 NIV

After defibrillation, a groan escaped my lips as I struggled to open my eyes. "We have a pulse. She's conscious," the voice said as the burning sensation intensified in my chest. As I faded in and out of consciousness, pain wracked my body in waves. *I must still be inside the house*, I said to myself.

I faintly remember feeling the straps being placed across my chest as different voices called out my vital signs. Heated pain engulfed every pore of my body before everything faded out once again.

It's raining, I thought as I opened up my left eye and tried to figure out where I was and why there was an intense burning in my chest. I felt cool raindrops falling down on me, but somehow they felt comforting.

I heard a man's voice and the crackle of the radio, and immediately I felt pain all over my body. Pain raged from my head to my toes as I realized I was lying on a gurney. I remembered Jimmy had shot me.

A silent scream started deep down in my chest and erupted to the surface with the power of a great volcano. I screamed out in agony, not just for the pain I was in but because I knew deep in my heart that this day was coming. I knew he was going to kill me, and I had been powerless to stop it.

What could I have done differently? Could I have prevented it? Why did my husband hate me so much?

So many thoughts went through my head. So much pain wracked my body. Everything felt surreal. I had come face-to-face with a stranger who had tried desperately to kill me. But I was alive, and I had every intention of staying that way.

I faintly remember my ride to Lance Madison Army Hospital, which coincidentally was the hospital where I worked. I was transported to my own job. I was a registered nurse there. I can't remember much about the ride, but I do remember arriving and a lot of people surrounding me, speaking in hushed but urgent tones.

I was in a lot of pain and crying out in agony over and over again. According to my colleague Nurse Henderson, the emergency room was packed that night. There were soldiers and spouses coming out the woodwork with a multitude of illnesses, but somehow they knew something traumatic was going on because *no one* complained about the wait. Most of them waited patiently for hours as my coworkers tried desperately to save my life.

Three bullets had entered my body—one in the face, the other two through my shoulder and in my left side. Two ribs were broken, and my lungs had collapsed as a result of the bullet through my side. The horrible pain I remember was from Dr. Stone repeatedly trying to insert a chest tube through the two fractured ribs into my collapsed lung.

Not really knowing what to do because they had never treated this type of trauma to the face, the doctors at Lance Madison made the decision to pack my face with gauze, hoping to preserve the soft tissue until I could be treated at Sims Thompsons Trauma Center. I loss a lot of blood that required numerous blood transfusions.

I went into respiratory arrest several times that night and kept coding over and over again. And they kept bringing me back to life. In fact, the intense burning I had been feeling in my chest was a result of being shocked back to life with the defibrillator.

I found out later that when the first police officer and paramedics arrived at my house, they found me unresponsive and without a pulse. CPR was performed and I was revived. It was a lot of teamwork at the scene. In my left hand, I held a knife that my husband had staged. I lost so much blood, and they had to keep pumping more and more into my body to stabilize me for transport to the trauma unit at Sims Thompson.

I have very vivid memories of the assault. As I write, it has been twenty-plus years, but I can't imagine ever forgetting. It was not a situation one would soon forget. That goes for me and all the people surrounding me who fought so frantically to sustain my life.

I can imagine working in an emergency room and being alerted of the pending arrival of a shooting victim barely clinging to life. In my mind, I am preparing instruments and briefing other staff members on what has been relayed from the emergency medical technicians and then the patient enters with blood and trauma to the face like we have never seen before. As I rush to transport the patient to the operating room, I hear a familiar voice crying out from beneath the trauma.

The voice is one that is so familiar that it makes me pause for just a second, and in that brief moment, it hits me like a ton of bricks. The person lying on the gurney, the life I am attempting to save is one of my own—my battle, my coworker, and my friend.

That is what happened on that unthinkable night in 1992. God gave my coworkers an awesome assignment, but He also equipped them with the strength and fortitude to put their emotions aside and put into practice what we had all been trained to do. Oh, how I thank God for His abundant favor!

My brave commander Colonel Andrews was a decorated pilot in Vietnam. He personally flew me in a helicopter to Sims Thompson Trauma Center. He wanted to ensure that I got there safely and immediately. I remember the ride, the excruciating pain, and hearing them contact the medical personnel at the hospital with my estimated time of arrival.

I fought to stay awake the whole time because of my head trauma. Colonel Andrews repeatedly told me to stay awake. I was also afraid that if I slept, I would not wake up, and I was not willing to take that chance. While we traveled, my medical team also contacted the thoracic pulmonary surgeon, Dr. Henry (who is my doctor to this day). He was on vacation with his family, but he didn't hesitate to fly in from vacation to treat me.

When we landed on the helipad at Sims Thompson Trauma Center, I was in pain from the top of my head to the bottoms of my feet, but I remember thinking, *This is my first time flying on a helicopter.* I was trying to distract myself from the chaos that was going on around me.

When we landed, there was a team of medical personnel waiting. I remember looking down and seeing many pairs of hands lined up side by side, sliding my gurney out of the helicopter. I knew then that I was going to be all right. It was as if those hands were a sign that God had placed me in the right ones.

After getting settled into the hospital, I was visited first by the ophthalmologist, Dr. Louders. She came in to examine me, and after assessing my facial injury, she made the quick decision to remove my right eye. It had been blown completely out the socket, and the nerves were severely damaged, leaving me blind in that eye. After she removed the damaged eye, she was able to save the vision in my left eye.

There were a lot of angels at work that night in the emergency rooms of both hospitals. I was given only a 10 percent chance of living. Truthfully, by the time they brought the plastic surgeon, Dr. Avers, in to reconstruct some of the facial damage, I firmly believe they thought I was going to survive. I dare not to say that they were trying to prepare me for an open-casket funeral!

Either way, their quick actions preserved my facial tissue, which made it possible to further reconstruct my face, so I thanked them regardless of my chances of survival.

But God had a calling on my life that not even three bullets from a .45 magnum fired at point blank range could change.

Silent Screams

The shout, the scream—
I always wondered why
I never heard the *sounds* of my voice, only
bullets in *whisper* passing by.
And pain and turmoil—a struggle for my life,
Inside a house confined to the wall,
Wrestling with a trigger. Not an escape to be found.
In shock. This is so, but I never heard a scream.
The gravely moments of torture, where breathing *slowly ceased,*
A warfare within me fighting to resist
The eternity dreads that lay ahead of me,
But a voice called out, and the foes departed.
And I realized that it was only my *Father.*
A warrior of *one stronger* than I ever felt
Stood beside me with keys of *hell* and of *death*—
And I survived.
Now *determined* to know more,
Why I never heard the screams of my voice.

Chapter 7

DEATH BE STILL

Are not all angels ministering spirits sent to serve those who will inherit salvation?
—Hebrews 1:14 NIV

I lay immobile for seventy-two hours in the ICU unit, breathing thanks to a ventilator. My body was swollen beyond recognition, and my skin had taken on a much darker hue. There were tubes running through my body, pumping in the good fluids and draining out the bad.

There was the distinct smell of gunpowder seeping through my pores, alerting everyone who came into my hospital room of the horror I had gone through. This foul smell was a constant reminder of the shooting for the next ten years. Whenever perspiration seeped from my pores, my body would give off that awful sulfur smell.

To the outside world, I was a trauma victim who lay unconscious, fighting for her life, but deep down on the inside, there was a mighty battle taking place for my soul! I don't know quite how to explain my near-death experience, but I'll just say out of view of the human eye, as I lay unconscious, I had a frightening yet comforting experience like no other.

I've not shared this with many people; however, as my body lay motionless, I literally watched a battle take place between good and evil, and I was the prize. There were four or five little creatures surrounding my bed. They danced around my torn body like I was their next sacrifice. They had beady, evil-looking eyes, and they communicated in their own language. They seemed so sure that I would soon be joining them, so they bopped around and did their celebratory dance as they waited for me to draw my final breath.

My God! But there was a statuesque, strong warrior positioned close to my bed. He stood guard over me at the head of my bed, never uttering a sound or moving a muscle. He had long, flowing hair that had a quality of transparency. It was a reddish color that I have never seen before, and I couldn't tear my eye away. I found myself staring at his statue-like, all-powerful presence, which made me forget that those imps existed.

He stood unmovable without ever making a sound, and I understood that he had been sent by God and he held the *key* of life in his hands. As much as those little creatures danced over my body, they never got close enough to touch me. It simply was impossible.

For years, I have thought about the warrior that stood by my bedside, protecting my soul. I tried to paint a clear picture of him in my head, but to no avail. Each time I try to remember, it seems like I can only see parts of the whole but never the entire picture. I can see the reddish hair, but I never saw his face. I've tried to describe him in human terms, *but* in the twenty-plus years since, I've accepted that he was (and is) not similar to any human I have ever seen.

I always knew there was but one explanation, but I was afraid my interpretation would be ridiculed, so I've lived with the experience buried deep down inside of my psyche. For years after the shooting, I was unsure of myself. I thought of myself as mutilated, unworthy, and ugly.

Who would believe God dispatched an angel just for me? It took many years, but I am now strong enough to shout it from the rooftops. *God sent me a guardian angel.* I might not ever be worthy, but my Father loves me so much that He saw enough in me to save me. He gets all the praise.

I believe that warrior was given the job of protecting my soul until I was strong enough to reclaim it. I was weary and truly in a dark place. I was on the brink of death. I wanted to live, but I wasn't quite sure how to. And I definitely didn't have the strength to do it for myself. So for those seventy-two hours, I was content to lay wrapped tightly in His bosom. Oh, what *comfort.*

Silent Comfort

I weep but with tears of joy,
Knowing that I feel the presence of the Lord.
My heart is overwhelmed as I lie in silent comfort
Wrapped in his presence so nigh.

Chapter 8

COME RAIN OR COME SHINE

Have I not commanded you? Be strong and courageous. Do not be afraid; do not be discouraged, for the LORD your God will be with you wherever you go.

—Joshua 1:9 NIV

Three days later I awoke, March 21, 1992, to find my biggest supporter standing quietly by my bedside, holding my hand. She had tears in her eyes as any mother would when confronted with the horror of seeing her child mutilated and in pain.

For a moment, I was confused about where I was and why I was in so much pain. I began to panic because my head was wrapped up like a mummy and there was a bandage covering my eye, but seeing my mother at my bedside comforted me.

She started praising God as tears fell from her eyes onto my bed, and then I remembered. I remembered everything about the night three days ago when my husband tried to take my life. I remembered the terror I felt and the pain that took over my body as bullet after bullet tore into my flesh. My hand instinctively went to my right eye.

I looked at my mother bearing the weight of my ordeal and saw the tears she shed for me, and I automatically knew my life would never be the same. I tried to find my voice, but hardly a sound would come. "Ma'Dear," I called my mother, who instinctively knew what I was asking.

"They're fine. Your children are safe. He didn't hurt them. They are with Toya and Denise," she said.

I felt an immediate sense of relief that they were safe, and I was able to relax and fall back to sleep. Later on that day, my sisters came to the hospital to see me and brought my children. I was so happy to see them, although I knew I was a gruesome sight to them.

I will never forget the wonderful feeling I experienced watching my sisters walk into my hospital room. Toya walked in first, holding my daughter Marian's hand, and she was followed by Denise and Ted, my son. Ted bravely stood in between his aunts.

The moment Denise laid eyes on me, she took a deep breath and fainted. She passed out on the floor and had to be transported to the ER. She knew I had been shot, but she was not prepared for the horrible sight and the foul smell. I had not looked in the mirror, so I had no idea what I looked like. I could only imagine what my children were thinking.

I could tell from the scared look in their eyes that I must've looked like a monster or something, but I was so happy to see them. All I could do was smile. I called them to come over to the bed. Marian looked like she wanted to run out of the room.

My daughter was visibly shaking and kept averting her eyes. She stood there with her hair in two ponytails, with eyes as big as saucers, but she finally came over and even climbed up on the bed with me. I was so happy to have them close to me and was sad to see them leave when visiting hours were over, but it gave me comfort to know my children were safe and in the care of my family.

After a few days, I was more alert and able to communicate better. I began remembering more details about the incident, and I learned about some disturbing events involving my children that took place immediately after my shooting.

While the police were processing the crime scene, my children were taken to my neighbors Adam and Barbara's house shortly after the shooting. Although I did not know them at the time, they reached out and provided a safe shelter for my babies after such a terrible trauma.

We had been living in the house for a few months, yet I had not formally made their acquaintance. My husband was opposed to my forming any type of relationship bonds with people, so I made sure to keep my distance. It was easier that way.

Adam, Barbara, and I had never done more than wave at one another in passing, yet they welcomed my children with open arms and gave them some peace for a couple of hours until the state worker picked them up.

Much to my horror, they had been picked up by my *mother-in-law* after that. She was the first person Jimmy called after he called 911, and she immediately came to the house since they lived only a few hours away. He requested that his mother go and get my children, and she did so.

I wanted to scream. How dare they? What had been his motive? He had attempted to kill their mother less than twenty-four hours prior, and he basically had no dealings with my kids. So what valid reason would he have to ask his mother to pick up my children and take them hours away?

Jimmy did not deal with my children *at all* after we married, so I was stunned to hear that he had sent his mother to pick them up after my shooting.

After what he had done to me, I could only surmise that his mom was going to try to intimidate them in some way to find out what they had witnessed or maybe even hurt them, and I thank God for not allowing that to happen.

My mother arrived the next day after the shooting, and when my commander, Colonel Andrews, found out my mother-in-law had taken my children to her home, he took charge and called her, demanding that she return them to Madison City immediately. She brought them back, and my sisters, Toya and Denise, and my mother took custody of my children for the duration of my recovery.

Praise Him

I will praise the Lord while I still have my being.
I will trust in Him. He helps and takes care of me.
He is my strength. My hope is in God.
God is an awesome God. He can do anything.
He feeds the hungry, causes the blind to see,
Heals disease and infirmities, delivers and sets the captives free.
He is worthy to be praised for His holiness,
grace, goodness and kindness.
God is my salvation, and I will praise the Lord forever.

Chapter 9

FROM THE MOUTH OF BABES

Before I formed you in the womb I knew you [and approved of you as my chosen instrument], And before you were born I consecrated you [to Myself as My own]; I have appointed you as a prophet to the nations. Then I said "Ah, Lord GOD! Behold, I do not now how to speak, For I am [only] a young man." But the LORD said to me, "Do not say, 'I am [only] a young man,' Because everywhere I send you, you shall go, And whatever I command you, you shall speak."
—Jeremiah 1:5–7 AMP

I was extremely worried about my children's well-being. I learned that they were able to run and hide in the master bedroom underneath the waterbed while Jimmy was assaulting me. God only knows how they managed to slip past him unseen and how they fit in that small space because the waterbed was only inches from the floor.

He never thought to look under the bed because it just wasn't apparent that anyone could fit underneath the bed, or perhaps he was too distracted trying to figure out what to tell the police about my assault. Whatever the reason, I am so grateful to God for keeping my children safe.

Mirian and Ted both remember lying quietly underneath the bed and watching my husband's combat boots as he went in and out of the room, looking for them. Ted told his little sister, "Shhhh," while they were underneath the bed, and she obeyed. It's hard to imagine a five-year-old and a three-year-old not crying after witnessing something so heinous happen to their mother.

I'm not 100 percent sure what Jimmy was doing in the bedroom while I lay on the couch dying, but Marian remembers hearing the waterbed shift above them. She felt like he sat down on the bed, and both of them recall hearing Jimmy telling someone what he had done. "I just killed my wife."

I believe it was that conversation between him and his mother that my children overheard while they were hiding underneath the bed.

I guess his mother was the person he called on when he was in trouble. But while he was calling his mother, I was calling on Jesus. He is the one I call on when I am in trouble.

Jimmy just didn't know the family he sought to destroy was covered by the *blood* of Jesus. Some days, I imagine my children cowering underneath the bed with a beautiful angel lying between them. Other times, I think maybe God rendered Jimmy deaf for that time period. All I know is there was a hedge of protection around my babies that God and only God could provide.

I cannot say enough about my children. Their bravery and resilience are astonishing. Ted was only five years old, and little Marian was three. They sat at the kitchen table while Jimmy shot their mother, yet they were brave and calm enough to seek out a safe place to hide. Ted will always be a hero to me. He saved his sister's life and his own by keeping a level head at his age.

Over the course of writing this book, I have come to realize that my son had a special connection to God that I did not see back then. He tried to communicate his feelings and visions to me, but I discounted a lot of it because he was only five years old. I've had to learn that God uses whomever He wants to use as a vessel.

It was a valuable lesson to learn, but I learned. Us adults have to learn to trust God, even when His messenger is a babe. It's been a rough twenty-plus years for my children. This event had a lifelong effect on both of their lives, but we believe in God's power. He brought us to it, but He also brought us through it. God gets all the praise.

When I think back to God's goodness, my soul rejoices. I survived. *Hallelujah.* I was alive, and even though those bullets had done a wealth of damage, God sustained me. In doing so, I knew very early on that He saved me for a reason. I was able to smile because I knew as long as there was life left in my body, I could overcome anything, and that became my mantra. I found out that the fourth bullet locked in the chamber of the gun. There is nothing my God can't do.

Those first three weeks in the hospital were rough. I went through multiple surgeries. My assailant's bullets did not kill me, but they caused a lifetime of damage. I had a rib resection to fix the two misplaced ribs and many surgeries to repair my sinuses, eye, cheekbone, and nose, and those were just the beginning.

I was discharged from Sims Medical Center in good spirits despite all the surgeries, pain, and trauma I had experienced. I was alive. My mother and sisters had my children, and according to the assistant district attorney in charge of my case, Alvin Campbell, Jimmy was going to stand trial for shooting me.

I met Assistant District Attorney Alvin Campbell while I was still in the hospital. At the time of my shooting, he was two years out of law school and was in the process of relocating to Madison. He was a young lawyer full of fire when the worst case of assault he had ever prosecuted was placed in his hands. He remembers my case being one of the more heinous and serious crimes he had ever taken part in prosecuting, and it was his greatest desire to see my husband pay for his crime against me.

I still remember the comfort I felt after talking to him the first time. He told me, "Ann, he's not going to get away with what he did to you."

Attorney Campbell worked diligently with the lead detective on the case, Raymond Owens, and the Madison Police Department to prove my shooting was unprovoked and not at all a case of Jimmy shooting me in self-defense as he claimed.

Years after the shooting, Attorney Campbell told me after viewing the crime scene video made by the MPD, he sat speechless. One thing that stood out in his mind and also spurned on his desire to see that justice was served was the callousness of the crime. When the video cut to the dinner table, Alvin could see I had spent the afternoon preparing dinner for my family; but mainly, his thoughts were of my children. *There were children present. He shot her in front of her children. He didn't care about the pain it would cause them to witness something like that.*

Keeping my children in mind, Campbell and his team worked tirelessly to make sure my assault did not go unpunished. Jimmy was released on bond after two weeks of detainment, but he was arraigned on charges of domestic battery. For me to press charges, the law required the victim (me) lost the use of a limb as a result of the assault, and I had lost an eye, nasal septum, cheekbone, sinuses tear duct and the use of a lung because of the shooting.

Despite the fact that he tried to blame me for the shooting, saying that I had attacked him with a knife, Detective Owens and the other detectives were able to recreate the crime scene to prove that was not the case, and they worked hard to make sure he was convicted for his crime.

Jimmy was determined to make me pay for calling the police, but because of his unwarranted hatred, there was a price *he* had to pay for trying to kill me.

So, as I prepared to leave Sims Thompson Medical Center, I appreciated the small things. I may have lost a lot of important things, but I was grateful for the little things that remained. I had lost an eye, but my vision remained. I had lost part of my face, but it was repairable. I had lost part of my nose, but thank God I could still breathe. There was a sweet fragrance in the atmosphere. It was *air*, and as long as I could breathe it, life was good.

Sweet Fragrance of Air

Sweet fragrance of air
I smell.
Where does it come from?
I cannot tell.
Maybe over the
yonder hill,
I say.
Sweet fragrance of air
So far away—
Most holy in the midst of day.

Chapter 10

A RAY OF HOPE

Though you have made me see troubles, man and bitter, you will restore my life again; from the depths of the earth you will again bring me up. You will increase my honor and comfort me once more.

—Psalm 71:20–21 NIV

After I was discharged on April 10, 1992, from Sims Thompson Medical Center, I was flown to the Greater Northwest Military Medical Center in Maryland. This was where the nation's soldiers went to be healed. It boasts the best of the best in terms of medical treatment for service members who are on active duty, retirees, veterans, war heroes, and their families.

I was indeed a soldier, an army nurse reservist from 1979, and I have been on active duty since 1988, nine years after graduating from Howard University. College life had its ups and downs, but I loved being a student. I always had a thirst for knowledge, and Howard University provided all the rigor I could stand.

It wasn't easy, but I endured the college's demanding four-year nursing program and graduated. Shortly thereafter, I relocated to be near my big sister, Sara, and her family, and I began practicing nursing in a hospital near our home.

I loved being a nurse, but I also had a desire to get out and see the world. I had already given birth to my first child, a son named Ted, whom I named after my favorite uncle. Eventually, my daughter, Marian, came along. My relationship with my children's father did not work out, and my greatest desire was to provide for the needs of my young ones. Shelter, medical care, and proper schooling beyond the basic necessities were high on my priority list. I wanted them to have a good life.

I visited a recruiter at Fort Vince, which was not far from my home. After careful consideration and weighing my options, I took the oath and became a commissioned officer in the US Army. I worked my way up the chain. I absolutely loved having the opportunity to serve my country.

My first active-duty station was Fort Madison, which is located outside of Madison City. The entire area, including the military base, had a population of about eight thousand. With my small-town ways, I fit into this quiet little setting quite nicely.

I became a registered nurse at Fort Madison's new state-of-the-art medical facility, Lance Madison Hospital. The new facility was a beautiful hospital, and I was thrilled to practice and hone my craft in such an innovative, modern building. I was a proud soldier and had no regrets about my decision to join the army.

I loved my job and received tremendous satisfaction from helping my fellow soldiers and their families. I was from a small town, and being a good steward and helping others was a large part of my makeup.

While stationed at Fort Madison, we lived on a nice residential street lined with single-family homes in Madison City. The majority of my neighbors were military families, and I really liked the neighborhood. My children were flourishing and seemed to like the area as much as I did.

I had been stationed at Fort Madison for almost three years when I met the man who would change my life in the most unimaginable and horrific way possible. He lived down the street from our house, and he began to take notice of me and my children.

Jimmy seemed very confident and sure of himself in contrast to my quiet ways, but I just assumed he was that way because of his position in the army and the fact that he was probably used to being in charge. He was very nice to me and often gave compliments that made me blush, and I began to spend more and more time with him.

I was very naïve about the ways of the world. I was a small-town girl with big eyes and a heart full of love. I was ready to settle down. I had two children and was not married, which was frowned upon in those days, and my friends often told me I needed to find a father for my kids. My greatest desire was to provide a good home for them as my parents had done for me.

I wanted the sunny days, laughter, and the easygoing camaraderie, but most of all, I wanted the complete family unit—husband, wife, children, and a house with that proverbial white picket fence just like my parents had back in Mississippi. I think that is why it was so easy for me to fall victim to such an abuser.

Dora, Mississippi, was a town full of folks who worked hard for what they wanted. They worked the land, mostly farming and picking cotton. My parents, Ken and Doris Wilson, had seven children—Ken Jr., Sara, me, Tonya, Denise, Kelvin, and Toya, who is the baby of the family.

Our upbringing was very simple and honest. My mama rose every morning at five o'clock and got us out of bed to start our day. She always prepared homemade biscuits and syrup for us to eat and sent us out to make our way across town. If school wasn't in session, all the Wilson children would be working.

I remember the beauty of the morning glories in bloom as we made our way to the cotton fields, where we sang all day as we chopped and picked cotton for twenty-five cents a day. Around noon we could see the old pickup rumbling down the dirt road, coming around the bend with the lunch Ma'Dear sent by my daddy. We would sit under the trees in the shade and grub on some good ol' collard greens and corn bread and then get back to work until quitting time at five.

In our free time, we would do the things that most children do, like race in the front yard and roll tires down the lawn. Every Saturday, we would ride into town. Ma'Dear would go to the store to meet her friends, and we would go to the five-and-dime and spend the money we earned from picking cotton.

On Sunday, the family would attend church services and have a big Sunday dinner. The kids would play in the yard, and the adults would sit out on the front porch, sipping on sweet tea and sharing the week's small-town news. By nine o'clock every night, us kids had to be in bed to get some rest for the upcoming day.

Some nights, we would lay in the dark, whispering about our hopes for the future. My sisters and I had dreams that ranged from getting married and having children to becoming rich and famous.

I just knew two things. I wanted to become a nurse, and I wanted to move out of our small town and see the world.

This was the life of most of the people in our community. It was school, work, church, and whatever entertainment you could find on the weekends. There was very little by way of crime, but there was plenty of news and gossip. Everyone knew one another, and you could pretty much take your neighbors at face value.

Don't get me wrong. There were those who had their fair share of faults, like Ms. Annie. She would come to our house through the cornfields, staggering every step of the way. She was an alcoholic, but she never made trouble for anyone but herself. She always seemed happy and would dance around and jump up and down, entertaining everyone.

She drank from sunup to sundown. I don't think I ever saw her unhappy or sober. I guess alcohol kept her from facing whatever grim reality she lived in. She would wander in and entertain us for a while and then make her way back through the cornfields. Ms. Annie drank so much I don't think she even realized when alcohol began to take her away, but I did. Many people in town wanted to help, but her choice to abuse alcohol sealed her fate.

Everyone had their own story, some good and some bad, but in the Wilson household, my father held us up to high standards. Education mattered, and I worked really hard in the classroom and graduated as the James L. King High School class's parliamentarian.

We were raised to work hard and be honest and genuine in our intentions, and those ethics and morals instilled in me by my parents served me well, especially in my profession.

That honest, hardworking young woman raised in the backwoods of Mississippi is who I am. She is the person I was back in 1991 when I met and quickly fell for the self-assured, confident, enlisted soldier down the street and took him at face value.

Some might say that my naiveté and upbringing opened me up to a bad element, but I'm smart enough to know that nothing happens in this world without God's authority.

Like I said before, God knows me—my strengths, weaknesses, and the desires of my heart. He knew I had a great desire for a husband and a father for my children, and I'm sure He would've provided a *good* husband and father had I stepped back and allowed Him to prepare that man for me, but I was too anxious.

It was my anxiousness that led me to the wrong man, but I thank God for preparing me for the battle that I blindly walked into. I think He was preparing me since birth. So, I can say without hesitation that all those early mornings I spent chopping and picking cotton, the carefree sunny afternoons spent laughing and rolling tires on the lawn with my siblings, and the long evenings studying into the night may have shielded me from the ugliness in the world, but it gave me determination and a zest for life.

My excitement for life made me want to live no matter what, and my simple upbringing made me faithful to God's promises, steadfast, and determined! And these are exactly the qualities I needed to continue living after my husband tried to take my life.

The Blossom of the Flowers

See the blossom of the flowers?
It is alive.
See the beauty of God exemplified?
And it is repeatedly seen,
For each season it renews and sprouts again.
See the blooming of its revelation?
See the glory of the Creator?

Chapter 11

A SEASON OF LEARNING

For everything there is a season, and a time for every
matter under heaven.

—Ecclesiastes 3:1 ESV

When I arrived on April 10, 1992, at Greater Northwest Hospital, I found myself in a whole new world. As I was wheeled through the corridors, I was surprised to see hundreds and hundreds of soldiers of all races in various stages of healing. Everybody there was injured or sick.

I don't know why I was surprised or what I was expecting to see, considering that it was a hospital, but I was shocked to see so many who were like me. They were missing limbs, walking around on crutches, or attached to IV pumps, and they all were dressed in hospital gowns.

It was all so overwhelming. The funny thing was that even with all the illness and disease surrounding me, I still felt like everyone was staring at *me*. I know we were all in the same boat, but I still felt like a freak show.

For the next five years, I would travel back and forth to Greater Northwest Hospital, where I would stay in three-week increments. However, on my first trip, I was hospitalized for three long months.

The bodily damage I suffered required extensive surgery and counseling. The specialists there told me I would only require approximately five corrective surgeries. Over the years that number has *drastically* increased, but that small number was the initial prognosis.

It was at Greater Northwest that I began undergoing major reconstructive surgeries on my face to try to combat the issues I had with my nasal passages and sinuses. I hated the surgeries because the anesthesia left me violently ill for days afterward. I would vomit until my body was exhausted, but there was nothing that could be done because the surgeries were necessary for me to try to reclaim some resemblance of my former self.

When I was there, I had to concentrate all of my efforts on healing my physical being. All the surgeries required to repair the internal parts of my face took a toll on me. The bullet tore through one side of my nose and exited through the other side, turning everything in between into mush. In addition to my nasal and sinus issues, there was the issue of my prosthetic eye. It was constantly causing me problems, and I didn't think it would ever get better because it kept falling out of its socket.

It was hard to even think about trying to heal emotionally because every time I looked in the mirror, I saw the nightmare I endured. I was convinced that I was a mutilated monster, and I was afraid to have anyone look at me. I used the black shades I had to wear to protect my eyes as a means to hide from the world. I went to counseling; however, for the longest time, I considered myself ugly and gruesome, and no amount of counseling could combat that.

I used to sit in my room, thinking about my children and my parents. I didn't worry about their physical well-being because they were in the care of my mother and my sisters, but I missed them and cried often. I worried more about what they had witnessed and how it would affect their emotional and mental health.

I worried so much about them, but I did not feel as if I would be able to help them because I was an emotional wreck. I was happy that God spared my life; however, I was in a deep depression, and some days I wondered if I would ever feel good again.

Some mornings, I would wake up with a renewed sense of hope and take meticulous care with combing my hair and making sure I wore the nicest gowns I could find in the hospital gift shop. I didn't want others to look at me and see the monster I saw, but despite all of my hard work, I was still convinced they did.

Being there gave me a lot of time to reflect on what brought me to that point. I was able to learn a wealth of information on domestic violence and the attributes of an abuser. I learned that abusers cannot love, so Jimmy never loved me. In fact, I believe he saw me as a potential victim from the start, especially since I was a single mother. He knew he could come in and provide what I was missing, namely a father for my children.

He was perfect in every way, showering me with gifts, and wining and dining me. By the time I met him, I was making a pretty decent income. I was well able to provide for my family, but he was the missing piece of my family puzzle. More than anything, I admired the fact that he was a first sergeant in the army and that he had his own money and would not rely on me for everything.

I figured together we could make a pretty good living and provide well for our family, but he wasn't thinking about the benefits we could have *together*. From everything I've learned since then and at the trial, I believe he was looking to benefit financially from my death. After all, he had also taken out a $50,000 life insurance policy on me at a little insurance company outside of the main gate.

I soon realized that there were many warning signs preceding my relationship with Jimmy. I just did not know what to look for, or rather I wasn't really looking for signs. I was looking for love. I was blinded by a *love* that was never really there.

In hindsight, some of the signs were spiritual, but most of the warning signs were bold and in living color right there in front of me. Others were behavioral cues and personality traits that domestic abuse organizations warn against. According to everything I've since learned about abuse and abusers, my husband was a textbook abuser.

His abuse of me was not the first time he had threatened, hit, or even shot at a woman. In the midst of beating me one day, he let it slip that his ex-wife was in hiding from him because he had threatened to kill her.

At first, I was skeptical about his story. Sure, I knew he would raise his hands to me, but for a woman to be so fearful that she was in hiding from him was unbelievable. However, I broached the subject with his mother, and she confirmed it for me on one of her many weekend visits.

After we married, Jimmy's mother, stepfather, and brother came down every other weekend and took over our household. His mother didn't try to hide the fact that she did not care for me. I don't know if it was so much *me* that she was opposed to or just the marriage in general. She let it be known on her first visit that she had certain expectations of her son. "My son gives me three hundred dollars a month to help with my bills and his brother's upkeep. I sure hope you or this marriage ain't gon' try to change that."

I let her know I had no intention of interfering with whatever arrangements they had prior to our marriage. That seemed to satisfy her; however, she still never warmed up to me, and the feeling was mutual. Whenever she would come, she would do Jimmy's laundry, make his favorite meal, and wait on him hand and foot. She always brushed me to the side like I was invading her space.

I remember standing in the kitchen with her one weekend while she baked Jimmy's favorite food, baked pork chops. I asked her about his ex-wife, and she gave me quite an earful.

According to her, while stationed in Korea, Jimmy's ex-wife was in a car accident. Reportedly, she was with another man when the accident occurred, and Jimmy threatened to kill her when he saw her. Afraid that he was going to hurt her, she never returned home.

When she was telling me the story, his mother did not seem the slightest bit concerned that her son was spreading fear into women's lives and threatening them. She was aware of his treatment of me, and if she ever spoke to him in my defense, I did not know about it. However, I doubt she did. In fact, on another occasion when she was cooking and I was in the kitchen with her, trying to figure out what she did so special to the baked pork chops, she made an offhanded comment that took me by surprise. I looked at her with wide eyes, praying she wasn't talking about me because the comment she made was frightening. She said, "Somebody's gonna die in this house."

Like the other warnings that preceded my shooting, I feel like her statement was one of the many cautionary signs that I ignored. I remember asking her, "Is it gonna be me?"

She just shook her head and said, "Oh no, it's not you," but why would she even make that statement in the first place if she did not have an inkling that something drastic was going to take place? Was she just trying to scare me, or did she know what her son was capable of?

I found out later that one of the reasons Jimmy's ex-wife ran was because she knew his propensity for violence. He had already shot at her before. He told me in the midst of an argument that I was going to end up like her and that I should go into the bedroom and look at the bullet hole in the box spring.

He claimed that he had tried to shoot her foot off and that the bullet had ended up in the box spring of the bed. Sure enough, there was a hole. I don't know whether or not the story of its origin is true, but there definitely was a hole in the box spring.

Thankfully, his ex-wife was able to escape before he really hurt her, and she was able to obtain a divorce in absentia. From there he moved on to the next unsuspecting victim or victims. I'm not sure how many there may have been between his ex-wife and me because I only learned of one during the investigation.

The detective on my case asked if I knew about the teacher living in the area he had dated prior to me. Supposedly, he beat her severely, landing her in the hospital, but her fear of him kept her from pressing charges.

I was shocked because the more I found out, the more I realized how little I knew about the man I had married. What I do know is that he ended up living down the street from me and my children, and from the day he came into our lives, I, my two children who were born before him, and the two children I had after, along with their children, have faced many challenges as a result of involvement with him.

Two Destinies

God rains upon the just and unjust.
There are two ways of life to enter: the wide gate with
A *broad* way that leads to destruction—
And many will be there—
And
The *straight* gate with a *narrow* way
That leads unto life—
And there will be few who find it.
God wants us to enter in at the straight gate,
Wherein He enriches, controls, upholds, directs and beams
Like a shining light.

Through It All

Through valleys low
And mountains tall—
God took me through it all.
When I was weak
And about to fall,
God held my hand and strengthened my heart.
God took me through it all.

Chapter 12

SKELETONS IN THE CLOSET

If we confess our sins, he is faithful and just and will forgive us our sins and to purify us from all unrighteousness.

—1 John1:9 NIV

On July 6, 1992, approximately three months after entering Greater Northwest Hospital, I was ready to leave the hospital, but not really ready. I was *cleared* to return to my home, but *I was not ready*. There were so many mental barriers I had erected in an effort to block out what had taken place. I was afraid of facing what had taken place. To admit it all would be to admit failure, and I didn't want to face the fact that I had brought that abuser into my home. It was a lot to digest.

The first sign of things to come happened when I returned to my home for the first time after I was released from Greater Northwest. I walked into the house alone and the first thing that greeted me was silence. After that, I noticed that *everything* had been removed from my home. There was nothing left except the broken green chair sitting by the window in the living room.

I later learned from my attorney that after posting bail, my estranged husband went back to my house as if he planned to stay, but he was told that he had to vacate the premises because the house did not belong to him. I had to give my mother permission to obtain copies of my mortgage papers from the courthouse to prove he was not the owner.

When the police made him leave, he took everything that belonged to him as well as many of my belongings. But what he left for me was an empty house that still bore my blood and tissue on the walls and in the carpet.

I don't know what I was expecting, but it chilled me to the bone to walk back into that house. I was quickly reminded of the horror that had taken place. I slowly walked around the living room, and my eyes were fixed upon the dark brown stains in the carpet and on the chair.

I didn't realize I was holding my breath until I walked into the dining area where I had been shot. When I rounded the corner into the dining room, I had flashbacks of the moment when I had braced myself against the wall after I had been shot in the face, and I began to shake.

As I looked around the room, I was immediately transported back to that terrifying moment as I watched Jimmy pull the trigger.

I don't know if I was in shock or what was happening, but I could not stop my eyes from looking all around the room. I could see a bullet hole in one wall and dried specks of blood all over the same wall, but as I turned toward the wall for support, I was confronted with the most heinous sight I had ever seen even in all my years of nursing. That wall was heartbreaking and horrendous at the same time. I saw my right eyebrow right in front of me, attached to the wall with greasy-like pieces of flesh dangling from it.

When I saw it, I became unglued. I let out a piercing scream and ran from the house, falling to the ground, overtaken by flash backs. I landed on the third floor of Lance Madison Hospital in the psychiatric ward! This was the first of my six mental breakdowns. Like I said before, I had no idea there would be so many barriers to cross before I could get back to me. I began a cycle that went from Lance Madison Hospital to Greater Northwest with no stops at my home for a long time.

After I was discharged from Greater Northwest, they would fly me to Lance Madison Hospital, where I would stay for further treatment. The facility became my second home, although I should say that it was my first home because I didn't return to the house I owned for a long period of time. I don't remember how or who orchestrated the cleanup, but the next time I stepped foot into my house, all the blood and gore had been scrubbed away, thankfully.

In addition to coming home to a clean house, my brother Kelvin and his brother-in-law came to Madison City to be with me when I crossed the threshold that time. They stayed with me for a couple of days, and I was so appreciative not to have to face those first nights alone.

I remember the day I spoke with my mother extensively about my future. I was having an extremely hard time putting the pieces of my life back together. I couldn't seem to make any decisions about how I wanted to proceed into the next phase of my life. I only knew one thing for sure. After the trial, I wanted to move out of my house. Perhaps I would go back to Mississippi.

My mother and I talked a lot during those days. She understood what I was facing and tried to be supportive of each step I took. When I broached the subject of moving home, she told me, "Ann, if you run away now, you are going to be running for the rest of your life."

Prior to that conversation, I really could not ever see myself being at peace in that house, but after praying about it, I decided to stay and face my demons. I decided to stay and fight for my life.

I had already been medically retired out of the army, and my future was very uncertain. I began looking around for organizations that supported domestic violence victims, but I did not have any success in the Madison area. The closest organization was in Sioux, and for whatever reason, I was denied assistance.

I was struggling financially and emotionally, and I really needed help. The Veterans Administration provided medical care and counseling, but when I applied for social security, I was denied. I was actually told that because I had a degree, I needed to use it, and I attempted to do just that.

I secured a job in a local hospital, but I had many difficulties. Aside from the physical limitations, I suffered from post-traumatic stress disorder (PTSD) and would jump at the slightest sound. If someone dropped something and it made a loud noise, I would break out in a cold sweat, and my heart would race. I could no longer respond adequately to emergencies, and the sight of blood upset me terribly.

And of course, there was the issue of having a prosthetic eye. Having vision in only one eye made practicing nursing hard. Keep in mind that I still had to wear the dark shades. In fact, I wore them for ten long years, and aside from that, when I attempted to go back to work, my eye socket had not yet healed. It would often leak fluid, which was a constant burden.

I was continuously wiping my eye, and my patients did not feel comfortable with me caring for them. It was very hurtful hearing the negative comments from the people I cared for, but I could not be angry about the way they felt. I will never forget walking into a patient's room to take her vital signs.

She was an elderly woman, and she didn't have a problem speaking her mind. When I went to the bedside to take her blood pressure, she looked at me like something was wrong. She drew back away from me and let me have it. "Uh-uh. No, you look like you need to be in this bed more than I do. Hmph. Looks like I need to get out of this bed and take care of you. What is wrong with you, child, wearing them dark glasses?"

I was so hurt. My self-esteem was already very fragile, and all I wanted to do was find a job to provide for my family. I wasn't angry at the patient because she was only giving her opinion, which was very accurate. I was a mental and emotional mess, and I could not adequately care for my own needs, much less those of my patients or my children.

I was eventually asked to resign from that position, and I spent many years working as a nurse's aide at a nursing home. It was a far cry from what I was licensed to do, but I could only do as much as my health and vision would allow. Leaving the medical industry was devastating to me. I absolutely loved nursing, and to have it taken away from me like that was just another nail in the coffin Jimmy had prepared for me.

Not Left Alone

I am left here to tell a story about domestic violence
And violence of any kind in itself
Greatly affecting the balance of one's being,
Also affecting one's perception of everything—
A situation so critical that it takes
God and God through others
Just to survive.
I am assured that if I had known beforehand
Of that deadly moment, I would have not
been here to tell you nothing.
I am grateful to God
Because He never left me alone.
That's why I am holding on to the hem of His garment
And I refuse to let Him go.

Chapter 13

JUSTICE OR INJUSTICE?

Vindicate me, O God, And plead my cause against an ungodly nation; Oh, deliver me from the deceitful and unjust man!

—Psalm 43:1 NKJV

On October 22, 1992, a jury of twenty-three returned a true bill of indictment against Jimmy Murphy. He was convicted of aggravated battery, a felony against Ann Wilson in a trial that lasted less than a week.

Despite the fact that he attempted to convince the jury that he shot me because I tried to attack him with a knife, evidence of blood splatters, location of the bullets, and testimony from myself proved otherwise.

In two separate interviews with police, the defendant gave two different accounts of what took place and what prompted the shooting in the home on Ridge Road. In the first interview, he stated that I came toward him with a knife as he stood down the hallway near our bedroom door. He fired one shot at me and hit me in the face, which caused me to retreat long enough for him to attempt to escape out the front door. According to police reports, Jimmy stated that I again attempted to attack him at the front door, so he turned and shot me again. After that, I turned and *walked* back into kitchen area.

The next day (after giving police permission to search the home), he stated that I was in the dining room and came toward him with the knife as he stood in the living room and attempted to leave the house. When reminded of the testimony he gave the previous night, he only replied, "I didn't say that."

The fact of the matter was there was no evidence of a shooting in either the hallway or the living room. There was no credibility in his testimony, and the jury was not convinced there was any justification in the shooting. Jimmy Murphy was found guilty of aggravated battery.

The official documentation reads,

> On the 18th day of March in the year of our Lord Nineteen Hundred and Ninety-Two, in the county of Madison did then and there unlawfully and maliciously cause bodily harm to Ann Wilson by depriving her of an eye and lung, members of her body, by shooting the said Ann Wilson in the face and chest; and did maliciously cause bodily harm to said Ann Wilson by seriously disfiguring her face by shooting Ann Wilson in the face.

For his crime Jimmy was sentenced to ten years without probation, but he only served a little more than three years. He was paroled for good behavior on May 6, 1996, and his probation ends on May 2, 2002.

At the time of his release in 1996, I was having surgery number twelve of more than twenty I would eventually undergo. While his incarceration was ending after three years, my injuries kept me imprisoned in my mind and body for many years to come.

I battled fear on a daily basis, and nights were even more frightening. Almost every evening I lay awake in bed, listening for the slightest noise inside the house. I often asked my daughter, Marian, to sit up with me. Together, we would watch television and eat peanut butter and jelly sandwiches until I would fall asleep.

My promising life was dramatically altered as a result of being abused and shot by someone I loved and trusted. The bondage in which I was living prior to the shooting paled in comparison to what I went through after being injured. These feelings only intensified when I was informed of Jimmy's pending release.

It was distressing to think that the man who shot me in cold blood was being released, and I immediately felt threatened. I still remember the feeling of being unimportant and overlooked when the chairman of the parole board told me, "Mr. Jimmy Murphy has paid his debt to society." At the time, I recall feeling like the law had failed me yet again.

Chapter 14

RECOVERY

Then they cried to the LORD in their trouble, and he
saved them from their distress. He sent out his word
and healed them; he rescued them from the grave.
Let them give thanks to the LORD for his unfailing
love and his wonderful deeds for mankind.

—Psalm 107:19–21 NIV

Marian

Not only did the shooting physically impair me, but it cut short a
very promising military career and left me suffering with numerous
emotional and mental impairments. And sadly, this tragedy had
lasting negative effects on the lives of my children, who witnessed
the shooting. Both Ted and Marian have had many years of therapy,
but they still suffer from PTSD.

For a period of time, Marian went through a rebellious phase and
had to be removed from the home. She spent time in therapeutic
foster care. She received more than a year of care from a local
family, the Sawyers, who provided a very loving and stable family
atmosphere.

Marian fondly remembers living in the home with this family,
which was blessed with a wonderful, nurturing mother who made
sure Marian was given all the love and attention she could stand. Her
foster father, Mr. Wilder Sawyer, was a spiritually strong and silent
type who made quite an impression on Marian.

One unforgettable memory she has is meeting Mr. Wilder in
the hallway one afternoon. With all the tragedy she had seen in her

young life, Marian had very little confidence, and she would often walk with her head downcast. On this particular day, Mr. Wilder stopped her and handed her a Bible. He gave her a Bible verse to memorize that instilled in the frightened young girl a goal to focus on while learning about the power of God. She remembers the words he told her years ago that helped to sustain her over the years. "I want you to learn the 23rd Psalm, and every time you pass me, I want you to recite it."

Marian took to the task very seriously and did not sleep that night until she had memorized the entire verses, which she recited to her foster father perfectly the next day and many days thereafter. She was always rewarded with a slight nod of his head. He wanted to let her know that he was proud of her. Once she was able to understand that these were not just words but God's declarations to her, Marian was able to rest in the comfort of these verses,

> The Lord is my shepherd; I shall not want. He makes me lie down in green pastures: he leads me beside the still waters. He restores my soul. He leads me in the paths of righteousness for his name's sake. Even though I walk through the valley of the shadow of death I will fear no evil, for you are with me; your rod and your staff, they comfort me. You prepare a table before me in the presence of my enemies; you anoint my head with oil; my cup overflows. Surely goodness and mercy shall follow me all the days of my life and I will dwell in the house of the Lord, forever.

For more than a year, Marian thrived in the Sawyers' household, but she longed to return home to us. She couldn't understand why she was the only one taken from the home.

Eventually, she returned to live with the family; however, after a short period, her resentment and fear of living in the house of her youth took a toll on her, and the rebellious behavior soon returned.

Marian was very angry after going through years of therapy with doctors who really didn't have a clue how to reach a young girl who only wanted to forget the tragedy that had taken place and live a

The Lost Sheep

Oh, my Lord—my Lord, where did I go wrong?
My sheep are scattered and left alone.
I am not at rest nor at peace
Until I find my precious sheep
That were given to me to guide and care for.
Now my sheep are scattered everywhere.
Did I not do what was told by You?
I first seek You to keep my sheep.
Somewhere I failed—but not for long,
For I have vowed to bring them home.

Epilogue

Within the comfort of my home, I have been able to find enough peace to raise my children to become remarkable individuals who are strong, ambitious, and compassionate. Surrounded by my children and grandchildren, I find comfort simply being a mother and grandmother who takes pride in the successes of my offspring.

I am an active grandmother of eight who has found a calling speaking out about domestic violence. Telling my story to the world has not been an easy task. Each time I share my testimony, I am transported back to that tragic day as if no time has passed. In spite of the emotional turmoil it brings, I am committed to continue speaking out.

As in the past, there are many who will pass judgment and find my story unbelievable. There are those who ask, "Why didn't you leave?" And there are still more who will continue to believe that I did something to make my husband shoot me.

I didn't write this book for them.

It is for the millions of victims of domestic abuse who need to see that there is life after the violence. It takes work, but there is possibility in the midst of pain. This book is also for millions of young ladies and men who are on the verge of falling in love with people who cannot love them back. Prayerfully, this book will educate at least one person on the warning signs.

This book is for the millions of people in this world who periodically forget that God commands us to *love* one another as He loves us. That means having compassion, empathy, and charity toward your fellow human. We never know what circumstances a person is living under.

Instead of passing judgment, we should learn to pray for one another and act in service to others, even if that means simply being a shoulder to cry on or a listening ear. We never know what remarkable results may come as a result of another person extending a small act of kindness.

Remember, if there is any suspicion of domestic violence occurring within any given setting, please report it. This brave action could be saving a life/lives with a peace of mind.

Those silent people remain an accessory to domestic violence.

9 781532 027536